MW01050874

THE WHIPPET WHO WEPT --- YODA'S STORY

Judith Toth Bigham

Copyright © 2013 Judith Toth Bigham
All rights reserved.
ISBN:10-1482614359
ISBN-13:978-1482614350

DEDICATION

To Yoda ---
Eric ---
And my beloved, Tom.

ACKNOWLEDGMENTS

Thanks, Mom, for helping me appreciate the magic, mystery, and majesty of the written word. Thanks for encouraging my juvenile attempts to write the "Great American Novel." Your saintly patience, most certainly, earned you a high place in Heaven.

Thanks, Eric, for your encouragement and example. Your amazing way with words is a gift. You have helped me discover and develop my own.

Thanks, Jo Ann S., for making me believe I could actually write and publish my story. You are helping me "boldly go where [I've] never gone before."

Thanks, Jerry S., Cheryl S., and Joey D. for your "technical support." I'd have been (and continue to be) lost without you. I sincerely appreciate your time and patience.

Thanks to the friends and family who have read some of my work. I am grateful for your valuable feedback and generous encouragement.

Finally, thanks, Tom, for pushing me to "do something with [my] writing." Your continuing guidance and inspiration have helped me come out of that "closet" I've been hiding in. Your confidence in me is, slowly, becoming mine, too. I hope you'll be proud of me.

PART ONE

Eric was sixteen-years-old when he decided he wanted a dog of his own. He'd grown up with Australian Shepherds and Border Collies --- herding dogs that were integral to the successful management of the flocks of sheep and ducks maintained for use in my Stockdog Training and Events business. He had learned how to work the dogs; could send one of them to gather the sheep or ducks when I needed the flock brought into the barn or moved into a different pasture. He was a good handler and appeared to enjoy working the dogs. I'd assumed he'd want his own stockdog someday, but instead, here he was, telling me he wanted a … Chihuahua! Whoa --- I was genuinely concerned that the herding dogs would not appreciate a Chihuahua in their "pack" (they often chased and occasionally caught and killed small creatures), so I strongly suggested to Eric that he consider a dog other than a Chihuahua.

One of my stockdog training students at that time had Whippets (picture Greyhound, only smaller) in addition to the German Shepherd Dogs she trained for herding. I asked if she'd bring one of her Whippets along when she came for her next herding lesson so Eric could meet the dog and decide whether he liked or disliked the breed. She said she would, so a week later, Eric and I met Passion, a beautiful, charming Whippet bitch. Eric fell in love with her "at first sight." She and he took turns chasing each other around the yard then tumbling together in the straw on the barn floor. He was smitten, so it was settled --- Eric would get a puppy from Passion's next litter, due in May 2000. I breathed a sigh of relief. I felt a Whippet would have a much better chance of fitting, safely and successfully, into our established "pack."

Since the Whippet would be Eric's dog, he would be responsible for everything pertaining to him (or her), including the puppy purchase price. At that time, Eric had been working as a "stockboy" in his dad's Used Work Clothes store, earning minimum wage. He really wanted that Whippet puppy, though, so with his dad's and my blessing, he got his first *real* job --- slingin' hamburgers at a nearby McDonald's. From his earnings, he made payments on the as-yet-unborn puppy, so, when the litter was whelped on the twenty-sixth of May, his puppy was already bought and paid for.

Eric had no desire to show his Whippet in any kind of canine competition. The dog would be his confidante and companion. Eric was seventeen years old, by then --- an age when he considered parents an embarrassment. His dog would become his "pour-out-my-soul-to" buddy.

The breeder chose the "runt of the litter," a fawn-brindle male with one blue eye, for Eric. When she brought the nine-week-old puppy to the farm and presented him to Eric, my son hugged the squirming puppy to his chest and proclaimed, "His name is Yoda." "Yoda?" I questioned. "Because he looks so wise, but funny, too," Eric answered.

Eric and Yoda bonded quickly. The puppy followed Eric everywhere he was allowed to go and pined for his young master when Eric was gone to school, work, or out on a date. Yoda would jump to the top of the loveseat and press his shiny black nose against the window, waiting and watching patiently for his master's return. When he saw Eric's vehicle turn into the driveway, he'd leap to the floor and run to the door, wagging his whip-like tail, furiously. Eric would be greeted with high-pitched "yips" of unbridled joy and showered with "puppy kisses" when he knelt to scoop Yoda into his arms. Whether Eric was gone for a few minutes or a few hours, Yoda's vigil at the window followed by the wildly joyful reunion never varied. Their devotion to one another was heartwarming and undeniable.

On the twenty-sixth of May, 2001, as we prepared to celebrate Yoda's first birthday, my husband, Tom, came home from work not feeling well. Two days later, in the hospital Emergency Room, we learned that Tom had suffered a massive heart attack. He underwent cardiac by-pass surgery on the fourth of June, the day after Eric's graduation from high school, which, of course, Tom had not attended. Eric was understandably traumatized by what had happened to his dad, and, following the surgery, Tom suffered serious complications which kept him hospitalized for several weeks. During that time, Eric continued to work at McDonald's, help out at his dad's Used Work Clothes store, and take care of the farm so I could stay at his father's bedside. Yoda became Eric's emotional support system, helping him find his way through the fog of an unforeseeable future.

On the eleventh of September, just two weeks before Eric would leave to go to college, the United States suffered the worst terrorist attack in our nation's history. Tom had finally come home from the hospital, and he, Eric, and I sat transfixed in front of the television watching the horrifying events of that sad day unfold on the screen. Yoda lay close to Eric, sensing the sorrow and anger each of us was feeling. When Eric came home from college in December and announced that he was quitting school to join the Army, Tom and I weren't surprised.

Eric enlisted in February of 2002 and traveled to Fort Benning, Georgia for Infantry Basic Training. During the four months he was gone, Yoda spent most of each day on the back of the loveseat, watching out the window for his master's return. When, at last, Eric came home on leave before reporting for duty at Fort Hood in Texas, Yoda was beside himself. Their joyous reunion was beautiful to behold, but, after just two short weeks together, Eric was gone again. Poor Yoda was so confused and distressed.

Eric didn't come home for Christmas that year because there were rumblings of an impending war with Iraq, so all active-duty military personnel were being kept deployment-ready. That war was "declared" in March, 2003. Eric's unit deployed to Iraq the following month (April). During that year-long deployment, Tom and I prayed, sent care packages and letters, joined a military support group, and prayed some more. Yoda knew something was wrong. He became especially attentive to my ailing husband. He would lay across Tom's lap and nap while Tom watched television. When Tom would get up and shuffle slowly to the kitchen to make popcorn, Yoda would follow behind. He'd stand with Tom at the microwave, waiting patiently while the popcorn "popped," then follow his "popcorn pal" back to the recliner where they'd share the snack. Every night, after Tom went to bed, Yoda would hop into the recliner, curl into a tight ball, and go to sleep, as close to Tom as he could get without sleeping on the floor next to the bed (Whippets, because they lack much natural "padding," aren't comfortable sleeping on hard surfaces).

When Eric came home on leave after returning from Iraq, Yoda's joy at seeing his master again could not be contained. Every fiber of his sleek, long-limbed body vibrated with excitement. His high-pitched vocalizations filled the air. His "pack" was together again and he was happy.

The toll that serving as a frontline combat soldier had taken on Eric was painfully evident. He was highly reactive to both sound and movement. Often, he would sit in sullen silence, staring into space, lost in the bitter memories of war. Yoda became Eric's "security blanket," giving our soldier-son the unquestioning solace and support he needed while he searched for his soul. At times, I would walk into a room and see Yoda wrapped in Eric's arms; Eric's head bowed and pressed into the dog's slender side. I know Yoda was giving our soul-shattered son all the comfort and courage his canine spirit had to give.

When Eric's leave ended and he returned to Fort Hood, it took a few weeks for Yoda to reconcile the reality of his master's absence, again, but eventually he relinquished his vigil at the window and turned his attention and devotion to Tom, once more.

Yoda had so much comfort to offer to those in need, I felt he needed the opportunity to do just that in order to survive and thrive, so he and I began making Sunday-afternoon visits to a local nursing facility. We spent most of our time there in the Protective Care Unit where those poor souls suffering from Alzheimer's and dementia were cared for. Often, the residents couldn't remember who I was, but none of them ever forgot Yoda. He was handsome, charming, and --- different. The residents loved petting his velvet-soft ears. They thought his blue eye was "magical." The nurses would wait until Yoda and I arrived to serve the residents their afternoon ice cream snack. Yoda would watch with rapt attention as each resident received a cup of ice cream. Licking his lips and with his ears lifted high, his eyes sparkled with delight when, at last, he, too, was offered a cup of ice cream. The residents giggled as they watched him push his slender snout into the cup and, with his eyes half-closed in blissful pleasure, slurp the sweet snack until every last bit of the treat was gone. As I held the cup of ice cream for him, I could feel every chilly exhalation of his breath on my hand. Yoda loved ice cream.

Eric was scheduled to deploy to Iraq for a second time in late 2005. Before that departure, though, his unit was given two weeks in September to spend time with family and friends. Once again, Yoda's "pack" was together and he was happy, but much too soon, the day of Eric's departure back to Fort Hood arrived and we were swallowed up in a flood of farewell tears and hugs. Yoda, sensing the sudden surge of emotion, became uneasy and began following Eric everywhere he went, even to the bathroom. The last one Eric said good-bye to before leaving home that day was Yoda. The bittersweet memory of Eric, down on one knee, holding his beloved canine companion in a lingering embrace, is forever seared into my mind and heart.

Although Yoda was saddened by Eric's departure, he no longer sat on the back of the loveseat with his nose pressed against the window, waiting for his master. Instead, he re-bonded with Tom, and before long, the two of them were best buddies, again.

Shortly before his second deployment to Iraq, Eric had met a young woman in an on-line "chatroom." They became friends, and as sometimes happens, their friendship blossomed into love. After surviving two tours of duty in Iraq, Eric was honorably discharged from the Army in January of 2007. In September 2008, he and his lovely young lady, Marissa, were married. After the wedding, the newlyweds took Yoda back to Texas to live with them. After all, he *was* Eric's dog. Tom missed his "popcorn pal" more than he cared to admit. I missed him too, as did the residents at the nursing facility. Then, just eight months later, Eric and Marissa brought Yoda back to Tom and me. The poor dog was emaciated and depressed. His appearance and behaviour were so alarmingly awful, I feared he might die.

"It's obvious he wants to be here with Dad and you," Eric said. "I guess he's *your* dog now, Dad."

Although he was overjoyed to be back home, it took Yoda several weeks to regain the weight and condition he'd lost while he was in Texas. Eventually, though, he was healthy and happy, once more. His bond with Tom grew even stronger. The only times the two of them were apart were when Tom was out of the house, either hospitalized or at a medical appointment. Otherwise, they were together --- sharing popcorn and watching television (Tom, often asleep, with Yoda, also asleep, draped across his lap). The two of them had created a game about whose turn it was to be in the recliner. During the day, Yoda was content to share the recliner with Tom, but at night, he wanted it all to himself. Precisely at eleven p.m. every night, Yoda would station himself next to the recliner and stare intently at Tom.

"It's not your turn, yet. The news isn't finished," Tom would say to the dog. At eleven-thirty, as soon as Tom struggled out of the recliner and shuffled toward his bedroom, Yoda would hop into the recliner and circle a few times before flopping down and curling into a tight ball. Releasing a long sigh of contentment, he'd close his eyes and settle in for the night. It soon became obvious that both Tom and Yoda enjoyed their nightly recliner routine.

In late 2009, I began to notice a definite decline in Tom's overall health and condition. He was becoming weaker; less steady on his feet. He was having trouble sleeping at night, so he was spending more time asleep during the day. His appetite was diminishing. He wasn't enjoying life much anymore, although Yoda never failed to bring a smile to Tom's face every day. As he had done for his master, Eric, Yoda became Tom's emotional support system, giving him comfort, joy, and unwavering devotion. He gave Tom something to look forward to each day.

In early February 2011, I was awakened by a strange sound --- Tom was grunting. I hurried to his room. The bedside lamp was on and the bedcovers had been thrown back. His elbows rested on the bed at his sides, but his clenched hands were raised toward the ceiling. He had a startled look on his face.

"Tom, I'm here," I said. "Everything will be okay. Can you tell me what's wrong? Are you in pain?" His wide-open eyes looked at me; his mouth drew into a tight "o" and he continued grunting.

"I'll be right back." I hurried out of the room and called 911.

"911. What is your emergency?"

"I think my husband is having a stroke," I answered calmly despite my racing heart.

After giving the operator directions to the farm, I hurried back to Tom's bedroom and found Yoda standing beside the bed looking up at his "popcorn pal." His ears were pressed flat against his head and he was trembling. I picked him up and held him against my chest. I could feel his heart beating as fast as my own.

"It's gonna be alright, buddy," I told Yoda as I laid my cheek on top of his head.

Please let it be so, Lord I prayed silently. When I heard the wailing siren of the approaching ambulance, I carried Yoda to the recliner and closed the door to the room.

The EMT crew determined that Tom was *not* having a stroke. Instead, he was suffering an "acute hypoglycemic event," which translates into a too-rapid drop in blood sugar. For a diabetic, like Tom, such an event could be fatal. The EMT crew stabilized Tom as best they could before pulling him onto a gurney to get him out of the house, into the ambulance, and to the hospital emergency room as quickly as possible. Just then, I heard Yoda whimpering behind the closed door. I opened the door to release him and paused to comfort and reassure him before leaving the house to follow the ambulance to the hospital.

I brought Tom home from the hospital several hours later. He had no recollection of what had happened to him. As we stepped through the door into the house, we were greeted by Yoda's high-pitched "yips" of joyous welcome. Tom smiled as he carefully bent over to pet the wriggling Whippet. Together, they made their way slowly to the recliner --- Tom leading the way; Yoda following behind. I brought up the rear, just to make sure Tom got where he was going without incident. When our little parade reached the recliner, I helped Tom sit down and get comfortable. Without waiting for an invitation, Yoda jumped into Tom's lap and draped himself across his lap. Tom began to stroke the dog gently. Yoda sighed deeply. I smiled, knowing that, for a moment at least, all was well in our little corner of the world.

Not long after the acute hypoglycemic event, Tom's appetite became an issue of concern. He was becoming nauseated every time he ate something, and as a result, began losing too much weight. A visit with his Primary Care Physician raised the concern that he might have gallstones. An abdominal ultrasound was scheduled to be done on the sixteenth of June to either confirm or rule out her suspected diagnosis. During the drive home from the physician's office, Tom was unusually quiet.

"Are you okay?" I asked. "My life has become one crisis after another. I'm getting tired of it."

My heart beat faster and my fingers curled tighter around the steering wheel *Oh, God --- Please don't let him give up. Help us get through this newest challenge. You've helped us through so much already.*

"It'll be okay, Tom. We'll just take one day at a time and do what needs to be done to help you feel better."

Whenever he wasn't outdoors going for a "doggie walk" with me, Yoda was with Tom. He sensed Tom's need for his presence. Yoda was the glimmer of light shining in the darkness shrouding Tom's days. He never failed to make his "popcorn pal" smile, somehow, every day. I began to suspect that Yoda was an angel in disguise.

On the sixteenth of June, after returning home from Tom's abdominal ultrasound appointment, I called a dear friend who was scheduled to undergo lung cancer surgery the next day. I wanted to assure her of my prayers and offer to help any way I could. Her son answered the telephone.

"Have your mom and dad left for the hospital, already?"

"They're not going."

"What?" I asked, confused by his response.

"Here's Mom," he answered.

Before I could say another word, my friend sobbed, "Frank's dead." The anguish in her voice tore at my soul.

"What?" I gasped. "I'm on my way."

Tom walked into the room as I was hanging up the telephone.

"Frank's dead," I told him. "I don't know what happened. Not sure when I'll be back."

Tom stood, shocked and speechless, watching me grab my keys and purse.

"Be careful," he said, as I rushed out of the house.

When I returned home a few hours later, I found Tom sitting in his recliner with Yoda draped across his lap, as usual. He appeared dazed and confused.

"Are you okay?" I asked, anxiously.

Tom slowly turned his head, looked at me, and with deep sadness in his voice, asked, "Why Frank and not me?"

PART TWO

Tom's abdominal ultrasound confirmed the presence of gallstones. Because of his existing health challenges, he was scheduled to see a specialist on the fourteenth of August to determine whether or not he could safely undergo surgery, should it become necessary. However, on the thirtieth of July, Tom woke me in the middle of the night. His breathing was rapid and shallow. His voice was barely audible.

"I'm so sorry to wake you," he gasped, "but I'm in a lot of pain."

I was out of bed and at his side in a moment. "Where does it hurt?" I asked him.

He pointed to his right side, just below his ribcage. I gently touched the area he had indicated with my fingertips. His sudden and sharp intake of breath startled me and I pulled my fingers away, quickly.

"I think you're having a gallbladder attack. I need to get you to the hospital right away."

Later, in the Emergency Room, Tom needed morphine to ease his pain. Lab work revealed an elevated white blood cell count, indicating infection. He was admitted to the hospital. After signing admission paperwork, answering countless questions about his chronic conditions, and, finally, making sure he was as comfortable as possible, I drove home alone.

Please Lord, I prayed, *Have mercy on my dear Tom. Ease his suffering, if it is Your will to do so.*

When I got home and stepped into the house, I saw that Yoda had urinated and defecated near the door. The poor dog was seriously stressed.

Two days later, on the first of August, Tom underwent "urgent surgery" to remove the infected gallbladder which had adhered to the backside of his liver, necessitating an abdominal incision after laparoscopic removal was unsuccessful. By the grace of God, and against all odds, Tom survived the surgery. When he was back in his room, a nurse attempting to make him comfortable, asked, "Are you doing okay, Tom?" My beloved husband, without opening his eyes, mumbled, "Did the surgeon find his watch?" "What?!" the very-alarmed nurse yelled. I leaned across Tom's bed and gently touched her forearm. "It's okay. There's nothing wrong. My husband has a really warped sense of humor." Her sigh of relief was audible.

While Tom was hospitalized, Yoda spent most of every day and all of every night in the recliner he and Tom shared, waiting patiently for his "popcorn pal" to return.

On Wednesday, the third of August, I called the hospital late in the evening to get an update on Tom's condition and to find out when he'd be coming home. The nurse I'd been speaking with said, "Your husband wants to speak to you." "Okay," I said. "I didn't call his room because I didn't want to make him have to move around too much, trying to answer the telephone." "He's sitting up in a chair watching television, right now," the nurse told me. "I'll go ahead and ring his room for you."

When Tom answered the telephone, we talked about this and that. Then, I asked when he'd be discharged and allowed to come home. "The doctor is planning to discharge me on Friday, if all goes well." "Yaaayy!" I cheered. "Yoda and I will plan a "Welcome Home" party." After a bit more "small talk," we wished one another a good night. Tom said, "Love you." "Love you, too," I responded and hung up the telephone. I walked into the room where Yoda lay curled in the recliner, his long snout tucked under his whip-like tail. "Yoda! Your "popcorn pal" will be home in just two more days!" Never moving his head, he rolled his eyes up at me and twitched the tip of his tail in acknowledgment.

The next morning, when I called the hospital to get an up-date on Tom, his nurse told me he was doing well and still on-track to be discharged the following day, Friday, the fifth of August. She mentioned that the Attending Physician had ordered Physical Therapy for Tom that afternoon, to help him "get moving" before being discharged, "... So, if Tom's not in his room when you get here this afternoon, just have a seat. We'll have him back in no time."

After lunch, and doing errands for my friend recovering from surgery, I returned home to check e-mails, telephone messages, and Yoda before going to the hospital to spend the afternoon with Tom. There were four messages on the answering machine so I pressed "Play" and listened.

"Please call the hospital as soon as you can. There's been a change in your husband's status." *Great!* I thought. *They must have decided to discharge him today instead of tomorrow.* The second message was, "There's been a change in your husband's status. Please call the hospital immediately." A quiver of fear crawled up my spine. *What's going on?* I wondered. The third message was, "You need to come to the hospital, right away … and bring your son with you." Every muscle in my body went rigid, my pulse pounded in my ears, and I could barely breathe. I felt numb. I couldn't think. I didn't listen to the fourth message. I went on "autopilot" --- I called our church.

When the Church Secretary answered the telephone, I identified myself and blurted out, breathlessly, "Something has happened to Tom. I'm leaving for the hospital, right now. Please let Father Ron [Pastor] and Sandy [Pastoral Associate] know." As I was rushing out the door, I saw Yoda standing there, trembling and looking up at me with anxious eyes. Without a word, I pulled the door closed and left.

I drove as fast as I could on my way to the hospital, wishing I could find a State Patrol vehicle to lead the way, but, no such luck.

Please God, I prayed, *Don't let this be bad..* Then, to Tom, I said aloud, "Don't you *dare* die without saying good-bye."

At the hospital, I ran from the parking lot into the building, rode the elevator to the second floor, and ran down the hallway to Tom's room. The room was empty; two maids were stripping Tom's bed. Before I could say a word, two nurses were at my side.

"Your husband has been moved the Intensive Care Unit. We'll take you there." In hushed voices, the kind nurses told me that Tom had collapsed as he was being escorted out of his room to go to Physical Therapy and had stopped breathing. After thirty minutes of failed attempts to revive him, he'd been taken to ICU and connected to a ventilator. Although the compassionate nurses tried to prepare me for what I would see when I got to Tom's cubicle, the brutal sight of his broad chest being heaved upward from air being forced into his lungs by the ventilator, left me light-headed. A young, dark-skinned doctor with a South African accent came into the cubicle and, with his eyes averted and his voice subdued, explained that an undetected post-surgical blood clot had traveled to Tom's brainstem, rendering him brain-dead. Although I nodded and responded calmly, "I understand what you're telling me," my wounded soul was screaming, *How can this be happening? He's supposed to be coming home tomorrow.*

After the young doctor left the cubicle, I began making the "notification telephone calls" --- first, of course, to Eric, then to other family members and friends. A young Catholic priest entered the cubicle and asked my permission to administer the sacrament, Anointing of the Sick. *Last Rites?* I thought. I nearly said, "No," but nodded. Sandy, our Pastoral Associate arrived before the priest was finished, so she prayed the appropriate prayer responses with me. As the young priest was leaving, Sandy asked his name. "Father Eric," he replied. ...

Shortly after Sandy arrived, Father Ron did, too. A nurse came into the crowded cubicle to tell us that a staff neurologist was on his way to exam Tom and determine the extent of the damage to his brain. After the neurologist arrived and performed the examination, he looked directly at me and asked, "Is everyone in this room a family member?" I hesitated, so Father Ron responded, saying, "We are her 'church family'." The neurologist nodded, then asked me, "Is it okay for them to hear what I'm going to tell you?" "Yes," I answered, without hesitation. Averting his eyes, the neurologist said, "Your husband has suffered

17

irreparable damage to his brainstem. He can't feel anything and he'll never be able to breathe on his own again. Do you understand what I'm telling you?" "I do," I answered, calmly.

Not long after the neurologist left the cubicle, a nurse came in to counsel me about the "terminating life support" process. I listened attentively, but felt detached from everything that was going on around me. Father Ron urged me to "Let go and let it out," but I couldn't cry. I felt I needed to be strong for all those kind nurses and doctors who were so distressed by what had happened to my beloved husband and were trying so hard to make an unthinkably horrible situation easier for me to bear. I couldn't think anymore, so it was decided that a brain scan would be performed the next morning to confirm the lack of brain function, which would, supposedly, make terminating life support easier for me. Before leaving for the night, I asked Sandy if she would come back to the hospital the next morning and be with me when ... . "I'll be here," she promised.

When I returned home that night, I discovered that Yoda had urinated and defecated near the door. The poor dog had been in the house, alone, all day. I cleaned up the mess without a word, then sat down in a chair and began to sob, uncontrollably. Yoda came near, tentative and trembling. I reached out and caressed his velvet-soft ears.

"Your "popcorn pal" won't be coming home --- ever."

I sobbed so violently, I became nauseated. I was trembling; my teeth were chattering.

I couldn't sleep that night. As I wandered aimlessly from room to room, Yoda followed. He stood beside me and watched as I re-arranged Tom's underwear drawer --- twice. Finally, just before daylight, I sat down in the rocking chair and closed my eyes. A short while later, I heard Yoda whimpering. Assuming he needed to go outside and relieve himself, I rose from the rocking chair and walked to the door, but --- he wasn't there. I found Yoda standing next to Tom's recliner. I tried to coax him into the recliner, hoping that being in it would bring him some solace, but he refused. Instead, he just stood there, looking at the empty recliner, whimpering mournfully.

On Friday, the fifth of August, I stopped to drop off some laundry at the laundromat on my way to the hospital. Eric, Marissa, and our six-month-old grandson, Jacob Thomas, were on their way. Eric knew that his dad might not be alive by the time he arrived, but he had told me not to let Tom suffer by artificially prolonging his life. Our son had become such a strong man --- Tom would be so proud. ... As I was pulling out of the laundromat parking lot, I received a call from the hospital on my cell phone. My heart leapt into my throat. "Hello," I answered tentatively. It was a nurse telling me that Tom's brain scan couldn't be done until later that day. "I'm on my way, so I'll be there whenever it's done."   The nurse acknowledged my response and advised me to drive carefully.

When I arrived at the hospital and went to the ICU, no one would admit me to the unit. I stood outside the double-doors separating me from my husband, waiting and wondering. Finally, a young nurse named Lisa exited through those doors and asked me to follow her to a small room near the ICU. She sat in a chair and invited me to do the same, but my back was so tense and painful, I chose instead, to kneel beside her chair. She took my hands in hers and said, "When I came on-duty at 7:30 this morning, Tom was fighting fiercely, and I was so afraid you'd get here and see that." I could feel the overwhelming emotion rising in me. I didn't want to hear what she had to say next, but she continued, "In his final act of love for you, Tom died on his own, at 8:58 a.m." The anguished moan that escaped my lips sounded frighteningly inhuman. I bowed my head and laid my forehead on Lisa's hands. She began to stroke my head. "When you go in to see him, now, he'll look peaceful. Your friend arrived shortly before you did and she was with him, holding his hand, when his heart stopped beating." I realized then, that even in the midst of misery, God's love, mercy, and compassion were made manifest. I'd been spared the terrible burden of terminating life support, and Tom's spirit had passed into eternity assisted by Sandy's presence and prayers.

Eric and his family arrived the following day after a grueling, straight-through drive from Texas. Yoda was overjoyed to see his master again, but confused by the stress and sadness he felt emanating from each of us. He was definitely distressed by the absence of his "popcorn pal," but Eric's presence brought him comfort and gave him a sense of stability despite all the chaos swirling around him. Also, the antics of the noisy newcomer, baby Jacob, provided a welcome distraction for all of us, although Yoda lost interest in the infant after Jacob thought Yoda's ears were pacifiers.

During the week Eric and his family were with us, Yoda and I managed to maintain some semblance of normalcy. Yoda had taken over the recliner, although he tried to be near Eric as often as possible. Eric, too, was comforted by Yoda's presence and would sit on the floor stroking Yoda's ears as the dog lay beside him, his slender head resting on Eric's thigh. It was obvious that they were still devoted to one another. On the day Eric and his family were leaving to return to Texas, Yoda began following Eric everywhere, afraid to let his master out of his sight. Inevitably, though, the dreaded moment of departure arrived. Eric lifted Yoda into his arms and pressed his cheek against the dog's slender body. "G'bye, buddy," he whispered. Yoda licked his master's hand gently. Eric bent over and let Yoda hop out of his arms, then straightened up and walked quickly to his vehicle without looking back. Yoda stood beside me as we watched our loved ones drive away.

PART THREE

The day after Eric and his family departed, I noticed a dark discharge draining from Yoda's eyes. I checked both eyes for irritation or infection, but there was no evidence of either. I carefully wiped the discharge away with a warm, damp cloth, but within a few hours, the profuse drainage was once again streaming down his face. On that same day, Yoda stopped eating.

The watery discharge from Yoda's eyes continued unabated despite my attempts to staunch the flow. A visit to the veterinarian confirmed the absence of irritation or infection. The veterinarian suspected an allergy and prescribed an antihistamine which I was to administer twice daily. After several days of treatment, though, there was no change in the condition. Then, it finally dawned on me --- Yoda was weeping. He was mourning the loss of his "popcorn pal," Tom, as well as the absence of his master, Eric. No doubt, that was why he had stopped eating, too.

"Yoda, you dear, sweet dog. I wish I could help you understand what has happened, here, but I'm as miserable, frightened, and confused as you are. We need to help each other get through this tragedy, buddy."

Yoda "wept" and refused to eat for exactly three weeks and four days. On that fifth day, the watery discharge stopped as suddenly as it had begun, and Yoda began to eat, again. Apparently, he had managed to accept and reconcile his losses and was ready to go on with his life. I, however, had barely begun my own "grief journey."

My life without Tom was challenging. After so many years of intense caregiving, I felt lost and confused. I didn't know *where* and *how* to direct all the physical and psychological energy I'd spent caring for my beloved husband. Then, I'd see Yoda curled up in the recliner he and Tom had "co-owned," and I'd feel a bit better. That dog became my link to Tom. As long as Yoda was near, I felt Tom was, too.

After Yoda regained a healthy weight and appearance, we resumed our Sunday-afternoon visits to the nursing home. The residents were delighted to see him again. Yoda was delighted to be getting ice cream, again. I couldn't help but smile as I watched that charming canine interact with his "admiring fans." Yoda brought so much comfort to so many in need --- including myself.

Seven months after Tom was born into eternal life, I suffered through an excruciating attack of shingles, brought on, no doubt, by intense grief, stress, and a totally-depleted immune system. Tom had died so suddenly, I feared that he might be feeling frightened, lost, and confused by what had happened to him. I yearned for some sort of sign that he was okay, but none came. Then, nine months after Tom's "transition," I was sitting at the computer in the room where he and Yoda had spent so many hours together in the recliner, watching television. Suddenly, I felt Tom's "presence" near me. Then, I heard him breathing --- a deep, steady inhalation and exhalation of air. A feeling of deep peace came over me and I breathed a sigh of relief. "Thank-you, Tom, Thank-you, so much., for letting me know you're okay."

I celebrated Yoda's twelfth birthday on the twenty-sixth of May. He was unimpressed with the celebration for the most part, although he definitely enjoyed the special treats he received. That date held significance for another reason, too --- it was the anniversary of the massive heart attack that had changed our lives (especially Tom's) forever. For more than a decade, I had tried not to dwell on that traumatic event, but I would never be able to forget it.

Less than three weeks after his twelfth birthday, Yoda began to die --- he stopped eating and drinking and began losing weight rapidly. He developed bloody diarrhea which led to severe dehydration. A visit with the veterinarian, which included x-rays and bloodwork, resulted in a diagnosis of Protein-Losing Enteropathy --- an intestinal disease characterized by excessive loss of protein into the gut, meaning the body is unable to utilize the protein it consumes. PLE is often the result of another disease mechanism (usually, cancer). Dr. Ellen, Yoda's primary care veterinarian, recommended further testing to either confirm or rule out potential causes, some of which (a food allergy or a specific parasite known as Giardia) would be an easy fix. However, further testing left us with more questions rather than the answers we'd hoped for.

"All of Yoda's lab results are good," Dr. Ellen told me. "He doesn't have Giardia or any other problematic parasites. I can't tell you what's causing the PLE, at this time," she said, sadly. "We'll administer fluids today to alleviate the dehydration and give him some anti-diarrheal medication as well as oral steroids to stimulate his appetite and relieve any gastric inflammation. Then, we'll just have to wait and see how he does." Holding Yoda tight against my chest, I nodded and whispered, "Okay."

Nothing we did made any difference in Yoda's condition. He continued to decline, becoming weaker and thinner with each passing day. Another x-ray revealed a slight thickening near the pyloric valve in his guts. Dr. Ellen suspected a cancerous tumor but Yoda was too weak to undergo any kind of surgery (biopsy) to confirm or rule out that possibility, so we continued supportive therapy and hoped for the best.

Watching Yoda suffer so was heart-wrenching. I'd lost my beloved Tom just eleven months earlier and now it appeared I was losing his canine companion, too. Yoda was the living link to my departed spouse. The thought of losing him so soon after Tom was too cruel to contemplate. On the night of July first, as I was crawling into bed, Yoda weaved his way into the bedroom and collapsed on the rug next to the bed. He'd abandoned his comfortable recliner to be near me as I slept. My eyes filled with tears as I reached down and ran my hand gently over his bony body. I wondered --- was he suffering the discomfort of sleeping on that hard floor for *his* sake ... or mine?

I hadn't told Eric about Yoda's critical condition. Since January of 2012, he'd been working as a Measurements-While-Drilling Field Technician for an energy services company and had been at a job-site in northeastern Pennsylvania for the past two months. Because there was nothing he could have done to help, I didn't want to upset him by telling him what was happening to his dog. I was hoping for a positive outcome for *all* of us.

During the night of the fifth of July, neither Yoda nor I slept much. I lay awake listening to his labored breathing. The poor dog was restless and uncomfortable, frequently struggling to his feet, only to collapse again. Each exhalation had become a long, drawn-out moan. I couldn't bear his misery any longer. I threw back the covers, swung my legs over the side of the bed, reached down and lifted Yoda onto the bed. I eased my legs around his emaciated body, cradling him carefully between my knees. Tears were streaming down my face as I lay back against the pillow and began to pray --- "Please, Lord, have mercy on us. Ease our suffering. Let this courageous creature cross the Rainbow Bridge, if that's what will give him peace and release him from the pain. I'm letting him go, Lord. Please don't let him suffer any longer."

Yoda relaxed and his breathing slowed. I relaxed, too. I thought our ordeal was over. Then, after what seemed like a very long time, I felt his ribcage expand against my knees. The inhalation was ragged and shallow --- the exhalation was a shuddering moan. My soul sobbed. ...

"Tom, take him. If there's anything *you* can do --- please don't let your buddy suffer like this."

"Yoda," I whispered, "please go. I release you. Go, be with your "popcorn pal." But, Yoda hung on, drawing one ragged breath after another. ...

The next morning, I called the veterinary clinic and scheduled an appointment for Yoda for that afternoon. I didn't know what else to do. I felt helpless and desperate. I needed some answers.

On the way to the veterinary clinic, I stopped at the cemetery. I lifted Yoda out of his crate and carried him to Tom's grave. I carefully put him on the ground next to the grave. He sniffed the newly-sprouting grass for a moment, then collapsed and stretched out on top of the grave right where Tom's lap would be. He sighed deeply and closed his eyes. My eyes filled with tears and I tried to swallow the lump of emotion that was rising into my throat. I knew then what I had to do.

"Thanks, Dearest, for helping me find the answer."

I gathered Yoda into my arms and carried him back to the vehicle with a heavy heart. He was so courageous and at peace with what was happening to him. I hoped that I could emulate his example, remembering what a well-known author and fellow stockdog handler had told me many years earlier, --- "Dogs could teach us so much, if we'd only let them." Hopefully, I'd learn the lesson Yoda was teaching me.

At the veterinary clinic, we were seen by Dr. Dave who had been consulting with Dr. Ellen on Yoda's case. He asked the Veterinary Technician who was assisting him to hold Yoda upright on the examination table so he could more easily palpate the dog's abdominal organs. I braced Yoda's hind feet so he wouldn't slip and slide on the stainless steel table, while Dr. Dave stroked the dog's bony back and ever-so-gently palpated his abdomen. Suddenly, Yoda winced and yelped, startling us. Nothing he'd endured thus far had elicited such a painfully dramatic response. The three of us comforted Yoda for a moment, then Dr. Dave said, sadly,

"There's a large, hard mass in there."

"Well, it's neither food nor feces," I responded. "He hasn't eaten anything for days."

Dr. Dave nodded, then sat down and looked up at me as I stood

27

close beside the exam table, holding Yoda against my chest. I could feel his strong heart beating.

"I know you don't want to think about this, but, Yoda's not going to get better and …"

"He's suffering terribly," I interjected, "and so am I."

I began to cry when I asked, "Should it be done, right now?" I'll never forget Dr. Dave's kindness and compassion when he shook his head and said, "Take him home and spend tonight saying good-bye. Bring him back tomorrow morning. We'll do it then."

"I want his remains cremated," I blurted out, "so I can put him with Tom."

Dr. Dave nodded. "We will take care of that for you."

When we arrived back home, I carefully lifted Yoda out of his crate, carried him into the house, and gently laid him in the recliner. He stretched out as much as possible within the confines of the recliner and closed his eyes. I noticed him trembling ever-so-slightly, so I covered him with a fluffy towel before going out to the barn to do evening chores. As I went about feeding and watering the livestock, my heart was breaking. First, my beloved Tom; now, sweet, gentle Yoda. So much loss in such a short time. …

Shortly after I returned to the house, the telephone rang. When I answered it, I recognized the voice of Yoda's breeder, my former student. I hadn't spoken with her for quite a long time and was somewhat surprised by her call.

"How're you doing?" she asked.

"Who told you?"

"Told me what?" she responded, cautiously.

"About Yoda," I answered.

"What's wrong?"

I began to sob as I related the painful events of the past three weeks, leading up to the heart-wrenching decision to euthanize Yoda.

"You know," she said, her voice quivering with emotion, "he was my favorite puppy in that litter. I called him 'my blue-eyed boy.' I'm so glad Eric was the person who got him."

"He was --- is --- so special in so many ways. Losing him, now, so soon after Tom, is ..." I couldn't say more.

After a moment of silence, she asked, "When will it be done?"

"Tomorrow morning," I answered. "I'm saying good-bye, tonight."

"Does Eric know."

"Not yet. He's on a job somewhere in northeastern Pennsylvania. I didn't want to burden him. I was hoping for a better outcome."

"Was there a reason you called me today?" I asked. "How did you *know*?"

"I didn't know," she answered, her voice subdued. "Something told me to call you ... and I did."

For a moment, we marveled at the timely coincidence --- or was it Divine Intervention?

"I'll be thinking of you and Yoda, tomorrow," my friend said. "Be brave."

Neither Yoda nor I could rest that night --- Yoda, because he was suffering physical pain; I, because I was suffering psychological pain. I spent the long hours talking to God, to Tom, and to Yoda, but nothing brought me any comfort. I was heartbroken about what *was* happening and what *would* be happening.

Early the next morning, Saturday, the seventh of July, I sent an e-mail to Eric

Dearest Eric --- I need to let you know that Yoda is scheduled to be euthanized this morning. He became ill (diarrhea; not eating or drinking) less than three weeks ago. Nothing Dr. Ellen, Dr. Dave or I did has stopped his rapid (and very painful to witness) decline.. At yet another vet visit yesterday, Dr. Dave was able to palpate a hard, painful mass in Yoda's abdomen (it hadn't shown up, definitively, on x-ray, altho' both vets suspected cancer). The clinical diagnosis was Protein-Losing Enteropathy caused by cancer. Yoda will be cremated so I can spread his ashes on your dad's grave, if that's OK with you. Please hold us in your thoughts and prayers, today. Much love always, son.

On that same day, a well-known and highly-respected Animal Communicator was scheduled to be at the farm to do consultations throughout the day. One of my herding students had organized and coordinated the event as a fundraiser for the farm. I'd never met that remarkable woman before and was, unfortunately, meeting her for the first time under tragic circumstances.

"Please forgive me," I croaked as I shook her hand. "I'm not at my best today."

After patiently listening to my tearful explanation about what was happening to Yoda, she asked if she could see him for a moment. Somewhat surprised by her request, I hesitated for a moment before answering, "Of course."

Yoda was lying flat on his left side in the recliner when Jen and I entered the room. He raised his head and looked over his right shoulder at us, then laid his head back down. Jen knelt down in front of the recliner, placed her left hand lightly on Yoda's abdomen, closed her eyes and lowered her head. I knelt down beside her and began to stroke his head.

"Yoda wants you to know he appreciates everything you've done for him. He's tired and doesn't feel well, anymore. He's ready to go, but wants to know if it will hurt."

I choked back a sob. "Tell him it won't hurt. It will be over in a moment, then he'll feel better."

Jen kept her left hand resting on Yoda's abdomen. "Yoda is telling me about popcorn. He says he really enjoyed eating popcorn and hopes he'll be able to do it again." I told Jen about the popcorn-eating ritual Tom and Yoda had developed. Jen nodded and assured Yoda that he *would* be eating popcorn with Tom, soon.

The next thing that amazing woman said left me speechless and in tears.

"I hope this won't upset you," she said, looking directly at me. "Tom is here, sitting in the recliner. Yoda is lying across his lap." I nodded, and finally managed to say, "That's how it always was. I'm so glad Tom is here with Yoda, now."

Jen began to push herself to her feet. Apparently, Yoda had said all he had to say, but, I needed the answer to one more question ---

"I've asked God --- and Tom --- to help Yoda cross the Rainbow Bridge so he wouldn't continue to suffer like this. I've given Yoda permission to go. What's holding him here? Why won't he GO?"

Jen lowered her head and closed her eyes once more. Several moments of silence, punctuated only by Yoda's shallow panting, passed before she opened her eyes, looked directly at me and asked, "Is there someone named Eric?" An anguished moan escaped my lips and I began to sob. "Eric, our son, was Yoda's first master. He was sixteen years old when he got his first job so he could buy Yoda. He lives in Texas with his family and is at a job in northeastern Pennsylvania right now. He doesn't even know there's anything wrong with Yoda. I just sent him an e-mail this morning telling him what was happening."

"Yoda is waiting for Eric," Jen said, quietly.

After Jen went out to the Meeting/Lunchroom in the barn to begin her animal consultations, I went back into the living room and knelt down in front of the recliner. I began to stroke Yoda gently.

"You dear, dear dog. What are you thinking? There's no way your master can be here with you today. I'm so sorry."

Not much later, as I was trying to eat some breakfast before taking Yoda to the veterinary clinic, the telephone rang. I took a deep breath to compose myself.

"Hello," I said.

"Hey." The sound of Eric's voice made me gasp.

"Oh, son," I sobbed. "Did you get the e-mail I sent you this morning?"

"I'm reading it right now."

"I'm so sorry, Eric. I did everything I could to save him. I think he wants to be with your dad."

"It's okay, Mom."

"Where are you?" I asked because his voice sounded muffled by unfamiliar background noises.

"We finished the job here, this morning. I'm on my way home to sleep-over before the long drive back to Texas."

"Oh. my God ..." was all I could say at that moment.

"What time is Yoda scheduled to be ....?" Eric asked.

"Ten-thirty," I responded.

"There's no way I'll get there in time." Eric sounded so dejected.

My pulse quickened as I realized the implications of what was happening.

"When do you think you'll get here?"

"I'm expecting to be there around noon."

"I'll call and re-schedule the euthanasia so you can be here with Yoda at the end."

"Don't let Yoda suffer on my account."

"I promise, I won't."

As soon as our conversation ended, I called the veterinary clinic. After identifying myself, I said, "You won't believe this ...." In a generous and compassionate effort to accommodate us, Yoda's euthanasia was re-scheduled to one o'clock that afternoon I knelt in front of the recliner, once again, and said, "You won't believe this, buddy. Your master is on his way to be with you when you cross the Rainbow Bridge. How amazing is that?" Yoda gazed back at me with calm, patient, *knowing* eyes.

At eleven-thirty, the telephone rang again

"I'm not going to get there by noon, after all. I misjudged the time," my son told me.

"What time do you think you *will* get here? Yoda's euthanasia has been re-scheduled so you could be with him --- at the end. Should I re-schedule it again?"

"NO," Eric said, emphatically. "Don't let Yoda suffer any longer. Do what needs to be done, for *his* sake."

"Okay," I responded, sadly. "I'll see you when you get here. I love you, son."

"Love you, too. Hug Yoda "good-bye" for me." His voice cracked with repressed emotion.

I felt desperate and angry. Was this some kind of cosmic joke being played at our expense? I needed some answers. Walking out to the barn, I waited until Jen had a break between consultations, then I confronted her.

"I don't understand what's going on. You told me Yoda was waiting for Eric. Against all odds, Eric is en-route, as we speak, but he won't get here in time. What am I supposed to do? Re-schedule the euthanasia? Go on as scheduled? What's going on here?"

Although my voice has risen in both volume and pitch, Jen had remained calm. She bowed her head and closed her eyes for a moment before answering me.

"Yoda can't wait, any longer. You've got to think of him, first."

"Okay," I said, my shoulders sagging with sadness. "I'll take him, now."

As I turned to leave the room, Jen reached out and put her hand on my left arm.

"Tom wants you to know that everything will be alright."

"Really?" I responded, sarcastically. "I can't imagine how."

Back in the house, I lifted Yoda from the recliner and, cradling his bony body in my arms, carried him outside to give him one more chance to feel grass beneath his feet. I walked slowly past several people waiting with their dogs for their time with Jen. None of them spoke as I walked by, but every one of them nodded with compassionate understanding. I carried Yoda to a shady, secluded spot behind the barn. He teetered when I put him down, but managed to get to a nearby tree where he somehow lifted his hind leg and attempted to "mark" the tree. However, he was so dehydrated, he was unable to pass any urine. I sat down on the grass and pulled my knees to my chest. Tears trickled, unchecked, down my cheeks. After a few moments of tottering around and sniffing the grass for interesting "messages," Yoda came over and collapsed beside me, panting hard.

"You are so brave, Yoda." I stroked him gently as I spoke. "I wish your master could have been here to be with you when you cross the Rainbow Bridge, but, you know that your "popcorn pal," Tom, is waiting there for you, don't you?"

The heat of the summer sun was soothing. Yoda closed his eyes as he lay, pressed against my side, and so did I. After what seemed like a long time, I roused myself and said, softly, "Time to go, buddy."

As I came around the corner of the barn with Yoda in my arms, my friend/student, Susan, the organizer of that day's animal communication event, stepped in front of me and said, "I'll drive." I nodded and gave her the keys to my vehicle. She held Yoda while I settled into the passenger seat, then gently placed him in my lap.

At the veterinary clinic, Susan knocked on the locked door (the clinic had closed an hour earlier). A Veterinary Assistant unlocked the door, invited us in, then escorted us to a room at the rear of the clinic which, instead of a cold, clinical stainless steel examination table, was furnished with a comfy couch. I sank into the couch and helped Yoda get comfortable in my lap. Susan sat beside me. A few moments later, Dr.

Ellen and the kind Veterinary Assistant entered the room and offered their condolences. Then, Dr. Ellen explained the euthanasia procedure before asking, "Do you have any idea when your son might get here? We could wait a while longer, if you'd like. Does he know where this clinic is?"

"Yes, he knows where we are. No, I really don't know when he'll get into town, but, he told me to do what needed to be done and not to wait for him. He doesn't want Yoda to suffer any longer."

Dr. Ellen nodded, then she and the Veterinary Assistant stepped out of the room.

Susan was stroking Yoda's head when, suddenly, she turned and looked over her right shoulder. When she turned back toward me, she was smiling.

"Tom's here. I'm sure of it. Yoda just looked at him."

"That would be wonderful," I said.

"Do you have your cell phone with you?" Susan asked. I nodded.

"Call Eric and find out where he is. If he's near, I'm sure Dr. Ellen would wait for him."

"Good idea," I said, reaching into my purse.

When Eric answered the call, I told him, "We're at the veterinary clinic. Dr. Ellen is willing to wait for you, if you're not too far away. Where are you, now?"

"In the parking lot."

"Where?" I asked, breathlessly.

"At the veterinary clinic. Now, I'm knocking on the door. It's locked."

"Oh, my God! He's at the front door!" I said to Susan.

36

Susan jumped up from the couch and told the Veterinary Assistant that Eric was at the front door, waiting to be let in. The young woman hurried to the door. Within minutes, Eric was standing in the doorway of the room.

"Hey, buddy."

When Yoda heard his master's voice, he lifted his head, wagged his tail weakly, and "chortled" his joyful welcome as best he could.

"You don't need me here anymore," Susan said. "If it's okay with you, I'll drive your vehicle back to the farm so you and Eric can ride back together in his vehicle."

Susan left the room and Eric took her place on the couch beside me. He began to fondle Yoda's soft ears. Yoda relaxed and closed his eyes, soothed by his master's voice; comforted by his touch. After several minutes, Yoda opened his eyes and raised his head. Eric turned and looked toward the corner of the room.

"What's he looking at?"

"Your dad is here --- waiting for him."

Eric nodded, turned back to his best buddy and resumed stroking Yoda's ears.

Dr. Ellen came into the room, greeted Eric, then lifted Yoda out of my lap and carried him out of the room to administer a sedative and insert a catheter in one of his front legs.

"I know this isn't easy for you, Eric, but, I'm so glad you're here. So is Yoda … he was waiting for you."

Dr, Ellen, carrying Yoda, and accompanied by the Veterinary Assistant, re- entered the room. She bent down and carefully placed Yoda into my lap.

"Are you ready?"

Eric and I looked into each other's eyes for a moment, then nodded.

As merciful, painless "death" flowed slowly into Yoda's body, Eric continued to fondle his dog's velvet-soft ears.

Thank-you, Yoda," I whispered, tearfully. "You were a blessing to all who knew and loved you --- especially, Eric, Tom, and me, too. You will live on in our hearts. Go now --- your 'popcorn pal' is waiting for you at the Rainbow Bridge."

Suddenly, there was an audible exhalation of air as Yoda's spirit left his body and sped toward his "popcorn pal" waiting to walk with him across the Rainbow Bridge. Dr. Ellen verified that his heart had stopped beating, then asked, "Do you need some time to say good-bye?"

Eric and I glanced briefly at one another, then he said, "No, we're good." Eric rose from the couch and tenderly lifted the limp body of his canine companion from my lap. He passed the body into Dr. Ellen's arms, then helped me up from the couch.

"We'll call you when his cremated remains are ready to be picked up."

"Thank-you --- for everything," I said.

As Eric and I were about to leave, Dr, Ellen said, "I have to say ... that was the most peaceful euthanasia I've ever witnessed."

I smiled.

"That's because the dear dog got what he wanted --- to 'transition' surrounded by those he loved most ... his master, Eric, his 'popcorn pal,' Tom, and me."

Back at the farm, I introduced Eric to Jen. Susan had already told her what had transpired at the veterinary clinic. As I turned to go into the house with Eric, Jen whispered, "After you left with Susan and Yoda, Tom told me that Eric would get there in time and everything would work out the way it was meant to."

"Well --- Tom was right. So was Yoda. By the grace of God, Eric was with us, at the ... beginning."

Jen just smiled and nodded.

AFTERWORD

Some would say that what happened on the sixth and seventh of July, 2012, was simply coincidence or an incredible alignment of events, but, it was so much more than that. I believe that love is the "energy" that links us to eternity. It was love that brought about a next-to-impossible series of events that blessed every person (and dog) involved. Samuel Taylor Coleridge says it best in his poem, *The Rime of the Ancient Mariner* --- "He prayeth best, who loveth best; All things great and small; For the dear God who loveth us; He made and loveth all."

THE RAINBOW BRIDGE

There are a number of versions of the poem and story, *The Rainbow Bridge*, said to be inspired by a Norse legend about the bridge between the realm of humankind and the realm of the gods (heaven). These poems speak of the patient vigil of pets as they wait in the in-between space between life and death, so that they may welcome their beloved human companions at the moment of their death, and cross the rainbow bridge to eternity together. Further information on the legend and the poems can be found through an Internet search.

)

ABOUT THE AUTHOR

Judith Toth Bigham has maintained a love affair with words since she wrote her first short story in a yellow lined writing tablet when she was twelve years old. She was "published" when, at fourteen years of age, she won second place in a patriotic essay contest sponsored by the local newspaper. Since then, she has had a short series on herding with a Shetland Sheepdog published in the *Sheltie Pacesetter* magazine, two essays published in the parish newsletter, several letters published in the local newspaper, and a few uplifting quotes published in *Guideposts* magazine. She participates in a monthly "Writer's Group" in an attempt to hone her writing skills.

After serving eleven years in the U. S. Army as a Military Musician, she worked as a Veterinary Assistant for many years before moving with her family (husband, Tom and son, Robert Eric) to an eighteen-acre farm in Nova, Ohio where she established (with the help, support, and encouragement of many) Hado-Bar Farm (named in honor of her first Australian Shepherd, Ch. Hado-Bar Jill, CD, STD-d). The farm has grown into a premier stockdog training and events facility, hosting many activities throughout the year, including clinics, competitions, and demonstrations. Recently widowed, she continues to maintain the farm (with the help of many).

27724964R00028

Made in the USA
Lexington, KY
21 November 2013